THRILL RIDES

VALERIE BODDEN

CAROUSELS

THRILL RIDES

VALERIE BODDEN

Creative C Education

Published by Creative Education P.O. Box 227, Mankato, Minnesota 56002 Creative Education is an imprint of The Creative Company www.thecreativecompany.us
Design and art direction by Rita Marshall Production by The Design Lab Printed by Corporate Graphics in the United States of America Photographs by Alamy (Chuck
Eckert), Dreamstime (Michele Loftus, Luna Vandoorne Vallejo), Getty Images (Ian Cumming), The House On The Rock, iStockphoto (Maya Kovacheva Photography),
Stephen Johnson, Shutterstock (Baptist, Jennifer Gottschalk, Rachael Grazias, Dee Hunter, Martina I. Meyer, George Pappas, Sergio Schnitzler, Juan David Ferrando
Subero) Copyright © 2012 Creative Education International copyright reserved in all countries. No part of this book may be reproduced in any form without written
permission from the publisher. Library of Congress Cataloging-in-Publication Data Bodden, Valerie. Carousels / by Valerie Bodden. p. cm. — (Thrill rides) Summary: A
colorful survey of carousels, including their seats and other features, descriptions of the ride experience, and a brief history. Famous carousels such as the Kit Carson County
Carousel are spotlighted. Includes bibliographical references and index. ISBN 978-1-60818-112-4 1. Merry-go-round—Juvenile literature. I. Title. GV1860.M4B64
2012 791.06'8—dc22 2010049378 CPSIA: 030111 PO1450 First Edition 9 8 7 6 5 4 3 2 1

CAROUSELS

TABLE OF CONTENTS

AROUND AROUND AND AROUND.

THE carousel spins. Its horses gallop. Riders love to feel like they are on a running, jumping animal!

A carousel is a ride that spins in a circle. Riders sit on carved horses or other animals. Carousels are also called merry-go-rounds. They can be found at amusement parks, fairs, and even inside buildings like shopping malls.

THE round bottom of a carousel is called the **platform**. The roof of a carousel is usually painted and carved to look fancy. Some carousels have only horses. Others have frogs, lions, or even sea monsters to sit on!

A carousel in England

YOU do not have to be measured to ride most carousels. You can just buy a ticket and climb onto your favorite animal. Then the carousel begins to turn! Most carousel rides last two or three minutes.

AS a carousel turns, its animals move up and down. On some carousels, the animals move forward and backward, too. Cheerful music plays. Some carousels glow with bright, colorful lights.

11

MOST carousels have only one level. But some have two levels, with one platform above another. They are called double-decker carousels. Riders can stay on the bottom level. Or they can climb upstairs to the top level.

A double-decker carousel

ABOUT 900 years ago, people in the **Middle East** played a ball game on horses. Later, people in **Europe** (*YOO-rup*) changed the game. They tried to catch a ring with a spear while riding a horse.

THEY practiced by sitting on wooden horses that hung from spinning bars. The bars were turned by people, horses, or mules. Later, **engines** were added. Soon, carousels became bigger and fancier.

Columbia Carousel

TODAY, the world's biggest carousel is the Columbia Carousel at Six Flags Great America in Illinois and at California's Great America. It is a 100-foot-tall (30 m) double-decker. It has 106 horses and other animals.

THE biggest indoor carousel is at the House on the Rock in Wisconsin. It has 269 animals! None of them is a horse. Every carousel is different—and every carousel can be a thrilling ride!

House on the Rock Carousel

Kit Carson County Carousel

ONE FAMOUS CAROUSEL

Name: Kit Carson County Carousel

Location: Burlington, Colorado

Year Opened: 1905

Platform Size: 45 feet (13.7 m) across

The Kit Carson County Carousel is one of the oldest carousels in the United States. It has 46 animals to ride, including horses, deer, and zebras. Some of the horses even have real horse tails! The animals do not move up and down. But the carousel spins faster than most carousels, at 12 miles (19 km) per hour.

GLOSSARY

amusement parks—outdoor areas where people pay to go on rides, play games, or see shows

carved—cut and shaped to make a design

engines—machines that use energy to make things, such as cars or rides, move

Europe—one of Earth's continents, or large areas of land, with many countries such as France, Spain, and Germany

Middle East—a large area of land between the continents of Europe and Asia, with countries such as Iraq and Egypt

platform—a flat floor that is raised above the ground

READ MORE

Rau, Dana Meachen. *At a Fair*. New York: Marshall Cavendish Benchmark, 2008.

Rosenberg, Liz. *The Carousel*. San Diego, Calif.: Voyager Books, 1998.

WEB SITES

National Carousel Association
http://www.nca-usa.org/census/census-psp.html
See pictures of carousels around the U.S.

Preschool Coloring Book: Amusement Parks
http://www.preschoolcoloringbook.com/color/cpamuse.shtml
Color pictures of all your favorite amusement park rides and activities.

INDEX